THE FALL

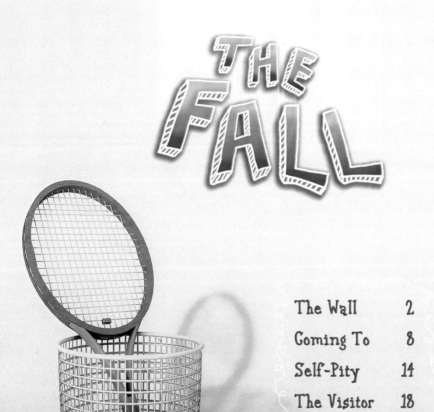

By Jack Gabolinscy

Illustrated by Adam Nickel

THE FALL

THE WALL

It happened between the fifth
and sixth floors of Zac's apartment
building. One minute he was the
fittest, fastest, strongest sportsman
in school. The next minute, he
was unable to raise his right arm
up to shoulder level, let alone
whack an ace in tennis or heave
a shot-put.

PREDICT

What do you think will happen
in this story?

...BETWEEN FifTH AND SixTH...

3

As usual, he was in a hurry, running and leaping down the stairs rather than going by the lift. Every now and then, he leaped onto the slippery banister railing and slid down on his backside.

He knew he shouldn't do it. He knew it was dangerous. He didn't need his mum to tell him how foolish it was. But he did it anyway. He liked to test his skill and his fitness, trying to beat the lift down to the ground from their apartment on floor 13.

He'd never beaten it yet, but this time he was super-determined.

Zac leaped down three steps at a time, sliding like an Olympic tobogganist on the railings. He'd never been so fast. He could hear the lift through the stairwell wall. He was ahead. He'd never been this close to winning before.

His competitive nature took the challenge eagerly. He gave it a bit more juice, a bit more speed, a fraction more daring.

Between the fifth and sixth floors, he leaped onto the railing. He landed perfectly, backside square on the slipperiest, fastest part. **Squeeeech!** Down he slid towards the next floor.

Zac had taken everything into consideration. He knew he had the speed and the skill; he knew he had the courage. He was going faster than ever before. He had everything under control. Well, nearly everything . . .

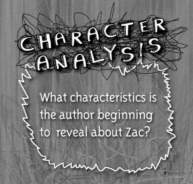

CHARACTER ANALYSIS

What characteristics is the author beginning to reveal about Zac?

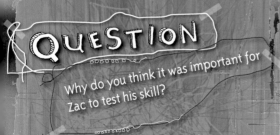

QUESTION

Why do you think it was important for Zac to test his skill?

LITERARY

simile
metaphor
personification

Are there any?

DEVICES

13

SQUEEEEECH...!

As he came down the banister, Zac looked ahead. There, coming up the stairs, just rounding the corner onto the fifth floor landing was a girl.

She was right in his way.

He was going to bowl her head over heels and flatten her against the concrete wall like a piece of squashed bubblegum.

Zac was going fast, but his mind was going faster. If he came off the railing, holding it in his right hand, and spun round the corner as he normally would, he would hit her hard. The only way to avoid her was to go over the top and hit the wall himself.

It was a no-brainer. Only one choice, really. In the split second before he hit the wall, Zac had one clear thought. "I should have listened to Mum!"

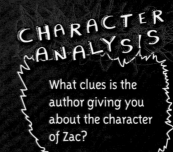

CHARACTER ANALYSIS

What clues is the author giving you about the character of Zac?

6

...ONE CHOICE...

CLARIFY
no-brainer

COMING TO

CLARIFY
trying vainly

Zac didn't have any more thoughts for nearly twenty-four hours. He didn't hear the girl's scream. He didn't hear the people gathering around him. He didn't hear the whine of the ambulance siren or see the glare of the lights in the theatre as the doctors worked on his battered and bruised body. He didn't know anything until the next afternoon when he woke up in a hospital bed. His mother and a nurse stood beside the bed, looking down on him.

"He's awake," said his mother. "Does that mean he's OK?"

"Can you tell me your name?" asked the nurse.

"Zac," replied Zac sleepily, trying vainly to lift his right hand up to his face. His eyes lifted to the drip above his head. "Why is all this stuff on me?" he asked.

"You had an accident. You're in hospital," replied the nurse.

"HE'S AWAKE!"

QUESTION

Why do you think the nurse asked Zac his name?

How do you know
Zac is regretting
his action?

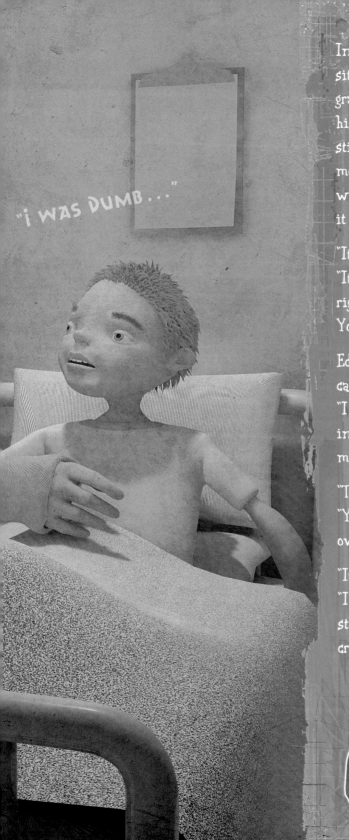

"i WAS DUMB . . ."

In a couple of days, Zac was sitting up in bed. The bruises and grazes on his face and around his ribs had faded a little and the stitched wounds in his head were mending, but his right shoulder was painful. He couldn't move it properly.

"It will take time," the doctors said. "It may not ever be completely right, but you're young and healthy. You never know."

Edna, the girl from the stairwell, came to see him with her mother. "I thought you were going to crash into me, but you flew right over my head like a bird," she said.

"Thank you," said Edna's mother. "You saved my daughter at your own expense."

"It was my fault," said Zac. "I was dumb, coming down the stairs like that. I was going like a crazy thing!"

CLARIFY

I was going like a crazy thing!

11

Zac's best friend Robert came to see him, too. He looked at all the plaster and bandages and laughed. "You look like Frankenstein, but don't worry. It's better than the way you looked before!"

Robert came every day after school. His constant chatter about everything happening at school kept Zac's mind off his sore shoulder.

"I won the tennis championship," Robert said awkwardly, when he came to visit one day. "I got the big cup. But it should be yours. You're much better than me, man."

"Not any more," said Zac sadly. "I won't ever play tennis again. My shoulder's too smashed up to play tennis. Or softball. Or throw the shot-put."

"No way," said Robert in disbelief. "You'll be as good as new in a few weeks. I betcha, man."

CHARACTER ANALYSIS

What kind of character do you think Robert is?

LITERARY

I betcha, man . . .

colloquialism or **slang**?

colloquialism = informal language that is often used in only one country

slang = informal language mostly used in speech and by one group of people

DEVICES

12

"NOT ANY MORE..."

QUESTION

What words would you use to describe Zac's emotions?

SELF-PITY

Two weeks after the accident, Zac went home. Most of the cuts and bruises had disappeared. His hair, where they'd cut it to put stitches in his scalp, was starting to grow again. His right shoulder, though, was still in plaster, still supported in a sling, still sore.

For the first few days, he stayed in bed, occasionally wandering out to the lounge to watch television, but mostly he did nothing . . .

When Robert visited, he cheered up enough to play computer games or to watch basketball or football on TV. But, as soon as Robert left, he curled back into deep and miserable thoughts.

His mum worried. "It's only to be expected," she told herself.

But, as the days ran into weeks, she knew that her cheerful, confident Zac had gone. In his place was an unhappy, silent young man whose moods hung over their home like a sullen storm cloud blocking the sun.

Zac didn't want to do anything or go anywhere. He didn't want to talk to anyone. He just wanted to sit and mope all day, mourning the loss of his strong right arm, drowning in self-pity.

"What if I can't ever play tennis again?" he fretted. "What if I can't swing a softball bat or toss a shot-put? What can I do without my sport?"

IMAGERY

. . . whose moods hung over their home like a sullen storm cloud blocking the sun . . .

What picture do you see in your mind?

How do you think the character
of Zac might develop?

...DROWNING IN
SELF-PITY...

CLARIFY

self-pity

"Hey listen, man," said Robert. "It's not the end of the world. Your arm will get better. It just needs time. Come back to school. You'll be right in no time, man. I betcha."

But Zac was trapped in a deep, dark abyss.

Nobody could cheer him up — not even Robert. "Leave me alone. Go away. I don't want you around here being a nuisance all the time," stormed Zac in one of his moods. "You hang around like a blowfly. Buzz off!"

"Snap out of it, Zac," said his mum. "You can't talk to your friend like that. Give yourself a chance. You don't know what your arm's going to be like until you give it a go. You might be surprised."

OPINION

Do you think Robert should have stopped visiting Zac? Why or why not?

"BUZZ OFF!"

LITERARY

simile
metaphor
colloquialism
slang
personification

Are there any?

DEVICES

16

CLARIFY
. . . trapped in a deep, dark abyss . . .

"It's no good," whined Zac. "I can't even lift my tennis racquet."

"Not yet. But you might," said his mum. "Besides, there are other things in life, you know. There's more than tennis. More than sport."

"But sport's what I want to do," grumbled Zac. "That's what I'm good at . . . was good at."

No matter what his mum said, Zac remained unhappy. He didn't want to go to bed at night or get out of it in the morning. He wouldn't go to school. He wouldn't go down to the park. He wouldn't apologise to Robert, who had stopped visiting him. He just sat around looking and feeling miserable, like an albatross with a broken wing.

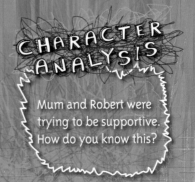

CHARACTER ANALYSIS

Mum and Robert were trying to be supportive. How do you know this?

THE VISITOR

One afternoon, Zac was lounging aimlessly about the flat when the doorbell rang. He ignored it. It rang again. "Mum! There's someone at the door," he called. Then he remembered — she had gone shopping. It rang again. Reluctantly, he answered it himself.

"Yeah, what?" he growled, jerking the door open. It was Edna from the fifth floor. She jumped back, frightened by his anger. Zac was immediately sorry he'd been so unfriendly.

"Hello, Edna," he said in a more friendly voice. "What can I do for you?"

Edna looked at Zac.

"My dad wants to meet you. He wants to say thank you."

"But I didn't do anything. It was my fault in the first place," grumbled Zac gruffly. "Tell him it's OK. I don't go out any more."

"He just wants to meet you. Please come and say hello . . . Please!"

"He can come and see me," growled Zac.

"No. You have to come to him! Please! Please! Please . . ." she begged.

CHARACTER ANALYSIS

How does the author show Zac's mood?

INFERENCE

What can you infer about Zac from . . .

"He can come and see me," growled Zac.

Zac looked at Edna. She had a face that could be read like a book. When she was happy, it shone, but when she was not it looked lost and lonely, like a dog-eared abandoned book.

He heard the pleading in her voice. But he also heard another voice, an angry voice.

"Don't go! Shut the door! Tell her to bug out!" It was a voice of self-pity and defeat.

"I can't," said Zac, half-closing the door. "Not now. Maybe another time."

Edna's face fell. "OK," she said dejectedly. She looked at Zac shyly. "I'll tell him you'll come some other time."

Zac watched her go. He felt bad, but what else could he do? He wasn't in any fit state to go charging off down the stairs for no good reason. Then he heard another voice in his head. "Would it hurt to go down? She wasn't asking much really . . ."

Zac walked to the top of the stairs. Listened. There was no sound. "Are you there?" he called softly.

"Yes," came Edna's voice.

"Wait," he called. "Wait for me. I've changed my mind. I'll come."

They walked together down the stairs. Edna looked up at him and smiled. "Thank you for coming. I knew you would."

Zac smiled back. He felt better than he had for ages. "How did you know?" he asked.

"Because you're nice," Edna said. "I knew you wouldn't stay angry long."

PREDICT

How do you think the story might be resolved?

LITERARY

simile
metaphor
colloquialism
slang
personification

Are there any?

DEVICES

CHARACTER ANALYSIS

Zac's mood has changed. Why?

INSPIRATION

PREDICT

What do you think might happen in this chapter?

LITERARY

simile
metaphor
colloquialism
slang
personification

Are there any?

DEVICES

Edna's front door was open. "Come on," she said and dragged his hand when he hesitated. "Dad's waiting for you . . . in his workroom."

They entered a small room with a wide window. In the middle, on a paint-splattered sheet of heavy plastic, was a big man with big shoulders and big arms. He was sitting in a wheelchair in front of an artist's easel.

"Hello! You must be Zac. I've heard all about you." He nodded at Edna. "She knows all the gossip," he said. "I'm Barnard Foster," he added, reaching out to shake hands.

Zac looked around the walls. They were a patchwork of paintings. Paintings full of sunlight and smiles that radiated warmth, happiness and hope.

There were portraits of street cleaners and sellers, bankers and bus drivers, children and old people. There were scenes of streets streaming with busy crowds, towering city blocks, river barges and rubbish trucks.

Zac looked at Edna's dad. His big face shone like one of the paintings.

He knew right away that he liked this man. "Hello, Mr Foster. I'm pleased to meet you." He went to shake hands with his right hand, but realised his mistake and, embarrassed, changed hands quickly.

Zac looked back to the paintings. "They're so cool. I wish I could paint like that."

"Anybody can paint," said Mr Foster modestly. "I had never even held a paintbrush until I stopped playing basketball."

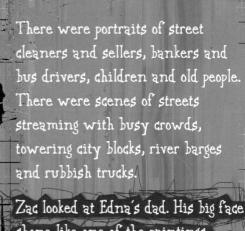

QUESTION

What do you think made Zac like Barnard Foster?

"You used to play basketball?" blurted Zac in surprise. Without thinking, he looked doubtfully at Mr Foster's legs. Then, again embarrassed, he looked away.

"My dad was a champion," said Edna. "Look!" She pointed proudly to a newspaper photograph, hidden among the paintings — in it Zac saw Mr Foster leaping to shoot a goal. Like a giant, he soared over the opposition players, high above the net. Below the picture, the caption declared:

"Breakers captain and champion goal-shoot Braveheart Barnard Foster shoots the winning goal for Bridgetown in the national championships."

Zac was dumbfounded. His eyes moved backwards and forwards between Mr Foster, his wheelchair, his legs, his paintings and his photo. "I . . . I . . . " he stammered, not knowing what to say.

Mr Foster interrupted Zac's mumbling. "I want to thank you for what you did for Edna. If you hadn't done what you did, she might be in a wheelchair, too."

"No. It wasn't like that," said Zac. "It was my fault. If I hadn't been silly on the stairs, she wouldn't have been in danger."

"You were still very brave," said Mr Foster. "Some guys might have done differently. You got a busted shoulder, but you've got a big heart. That's more important."

"My shoulder might not be so bad," said Zac. "The doctors say it will take time. It could get better." Suddenly he didn't feel despondent any more. "I think it will. I reckon I'll be playing tennis again next season."

"You can never tell what's in the future," said Mr Foster. "But you've only got one future. You've just got to make the most of it."

CLARIFY

despondent

INFERENCE

What can you infer about Zac's opinion of Barnard Foster?

CHARACTER ANALYSIS

Zac's mood has changed from despondent to positive. Why?

Later, on his way home, Zac was so excited he didn't even notice the weakness in his legs as he puffed up the stairs.

He felt as bright and happy as one of Barnard Foster's paintings.

"I'm going to ring Robert right away," he thought, running a few steps to test his legs. "I wonder what he's doing this afternoon?"

CHARACTER CHART

CONFIDENT

Zac before the fall

Zac after the fall

Zac at the end

THINK ABOUT THE TEXT

What connections can you make to the emotions, settings, situations or characters in **The Fall**?

taking a risk

doing the right thing

losing self-confidence

feeling depressed

Text to Self

having supportive friends

being inspired

overcoming obstacles

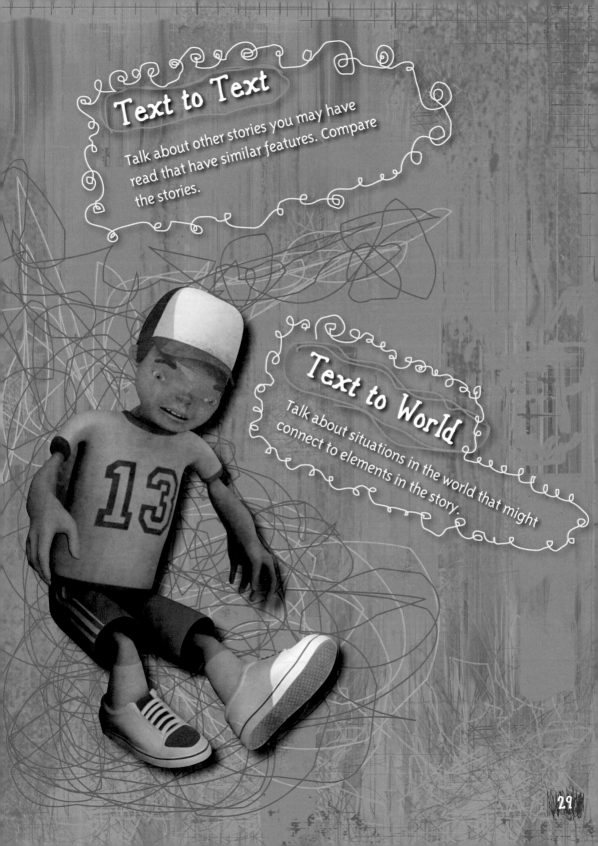

Text to Text

Talk about other stories you may have read that have similar features. Compare the stories.

Text to World

Talk about situations in the world that might connect to elements in the story.

PLANNING A NARRATIVE

1
Decide on a plot . . .

that has an introduction, problems and a solution, and write them in the order of sequence.

Climax

Build your story to a turning point. This is the most exciting/suspenseful part of the story.

Decide on an event to draw the reader into your story. What will the main conflict/problem be?

Conflict

Falling Action

Rising Action

Decide on a final event that will resolve the conflict/problem and bring your story to a close.

Set the scene: who is the story about? When and where is it set?

Introduction

Resolution

2
Think about . . .

major and minor characters
how they think, feel and act
their physical features
their voice and their way of speaking

3
Decide on the settings

SETTINGS

Atmosphere/mood

Location

Time

Words that
describe setting

Don't forget...

to write your events in order of sequence

WRITING A NARRATIVE

Have you...

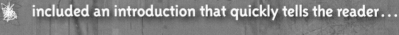

- included an introduction that quickly tells the reader...

  who the story is about

  where the story is set

  when the story happened?

- included a problem (or problems) that makes the reader want to read on to find out how it is solved?

- tried to create an emotional response within the reader?

- included description and dialogue?

- created mood and tension?

- included characters, settings and moods that are connected to create a believable storyline?

Don't forget to revisit your writing. Do you need to change, add or delete anything to improve your story?